# GREAT IDEAS FOR EMAIL

TAG

TAG Publishing

# CONTENTS

## THE EMAIL TEAM

**Illustration and design:** John Kelly
**Programming:** Paul Steven
**CD design:** Sam Webb
**Publisher:** Kate Scarborough

## Copyright and Acknowledgements

TAG Publishing.
a division of TAG Learning Ltd
9 Harmsworth St
London SE17 9TL

First published by TAG Publishing 2001
Copyright © TAG Publishing 2001

A CIP catalogue record of this book is available from the British Library

ISBN 1 902 804 05 8

Reprographics by Colourwise
Printed in Hong Kong by Wing King Tong

With thanks to: Cathy Tincknell, Tom Baird, Brian Boyd, and all the testers at TAG

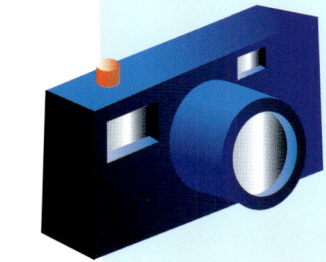

One of the most exciting things that your computer can do is send and receive messages around the world instantly. So instead of finding a piece of paper, an envelope and a stamp, you can type a note into your computer and press a button to send it to anyone else in the world with a linked computer.

## How does it work?

The key word when thinking about both email and the internet is 'network'. This is any group of computers that are linked together through telephone lines or cables. Because all these computers are connected, the information on them can be shared, and this includes emails.

You've got mail!

## What can it do?

As well as sending messages instantly around the world, there is something else that adds to the fun of email. You can send attachments - this can be anything from pictures, movies and sounds to puzzles and games.

4

## Great Ideas for Email - THE CD

The disc that we have supplied contains loads of ideas for attachments. You can create pictures, puzzles and more to send with your emails to friends and family.

**e-cards**

**e-music**

**e-cartoons**

**e-puzzles**

**e-pictures**

**e-codes**

## Installing the CD

**Windows**

* Click on 'My Computer' (your hard drive)
* Click on 'Email', which should show up in your CD drive
* Follow installation instructions

**Macintosh**

* double-click on the install icon
* Follow installation instructions

## Getting started

**Windows**

* click on 'start' on the task bar
* in programs, go to 'Email'
* click on 'Email'

**Macintosh**

* open your hard drive
* open the folder called 'Email'
* double-click on 'Email'

The most important thing you'll need to send an email is a computer linked to the internet. Check the specifications on the back cover of this book - you should have a computer that matches these or betters them. The more powerful your computer the faster both the CD and your email system will work.

*So, how fast can you download?*

## The extras

The essential kit you need to add to your computer to link it to the internet includes a modem (this makes information from the computer suitable to travel down a phone line) and a telephone line connected to the modem.

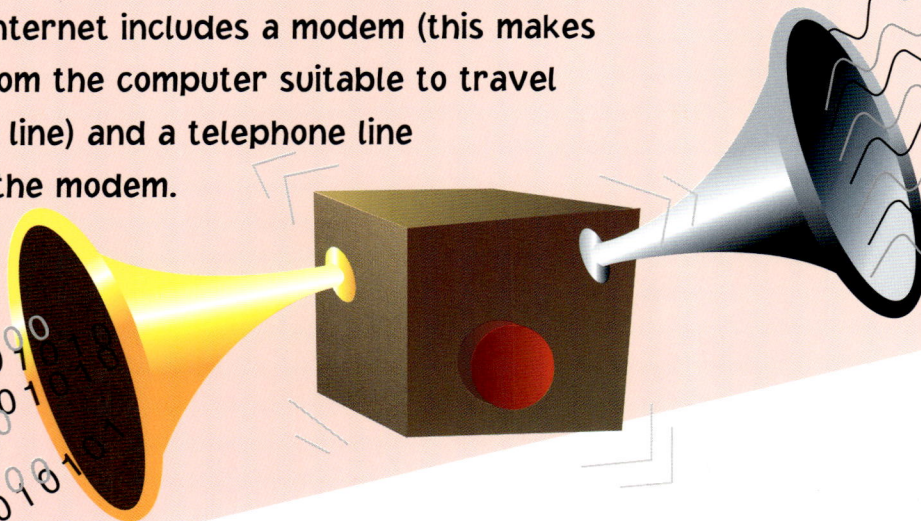

ISP

## Internet Service Provider

You also need to tell your computer how to link to the internet and you do this by installing software provided by an Internet Service Provider (ISP). The ISP links your computer to the internet through its own much more powerful computers.

## Email address

When you install the ISP you'll be given a user name and password – keep a note of these as they will come in handy. Sometimes they ask you to key in your own user name – this will become your email address, so think carefully about it before you enter it.

anybody@taglearning.com

# anybody @

anybody @ taglearning. com

co.uk

org

net

## An example of an email address:

anybody@taglearning.com. You can see that it has 2 parts separated by the @ symbol, which means 'at'. The first part is the user name and the second part is called a domain (home) name. You can have lots of user names with the same domain name, so at home everyone in your house could have their own address by putting their name first then the domain name.

*Most email addresses have no capital letters and use full stops (called dots).*

### What can you tell from the domain?

.co or .com means a company

.edu or .ac means an educational establishment

.gov means a government

.net means an internet company

.org means an organisation

www.greatideasfor.co.uk

There are many different email packages, some of which come with the internet browser you are using - both Microsoft and Netscape have email packages. Some email packages come free with CD-ROMs you get on the front of magazines. You can tell if you have an email package already installed on your computer because there should be an icon on the desktop, perhaps an envelope, letter or a mailbox.

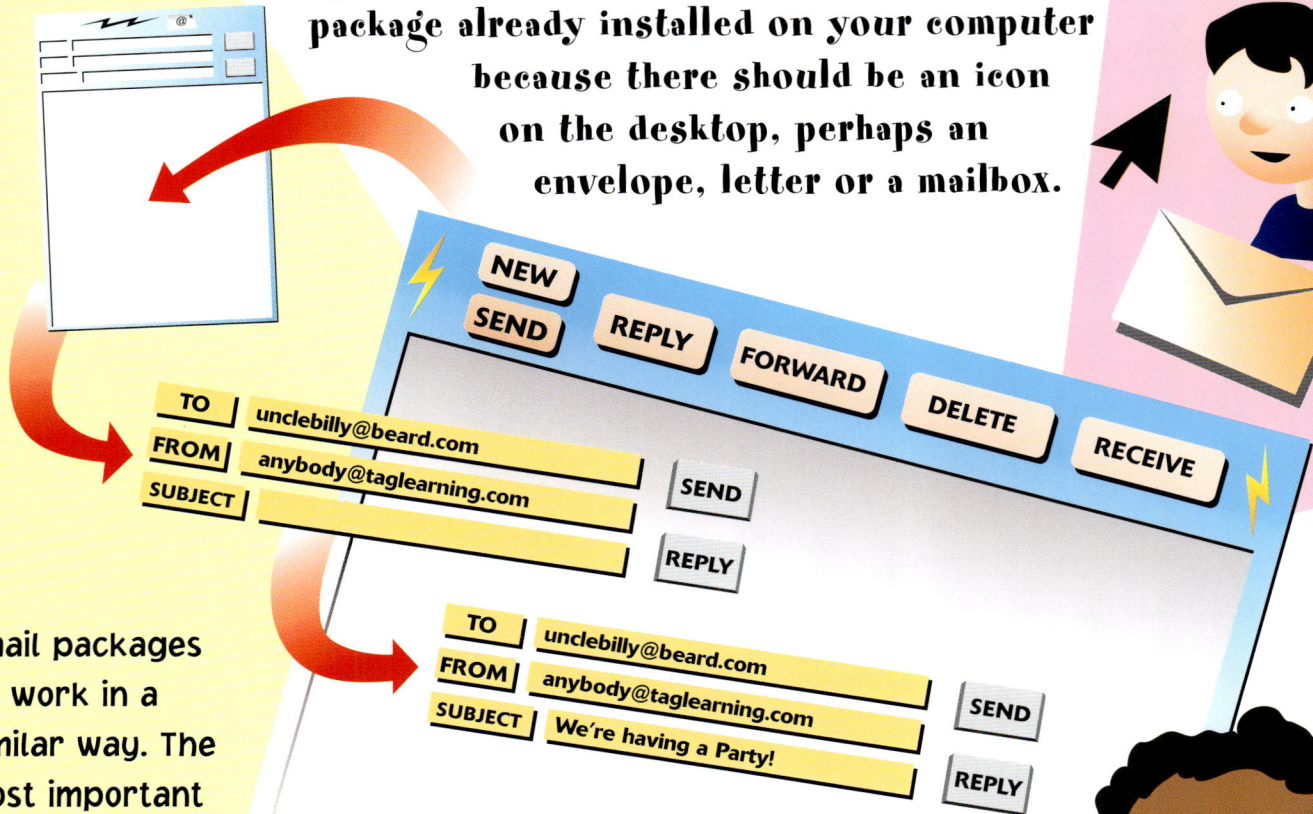

**NEW**
**SEND** **REPLY** **FORWARD** **DELETE** **RECEIVE**

| TO | unclebilly@beard.com |
| FROM | anybody@taglearning.com |
| SUBJECT | |

SEND

REPLY

Email packages all work in a similar way. The most important words to look out for are:

| TO | unclebilly@beard.com |
| FROM | anybody@taglearning.com |
| SUBJECT | We're having a Party! |

SEND

REPLY

**New** – this button should allow you to open a new message into which you type

**To** – this box is where you fill in the email address of the person you are sending an email to

**From** – this should already be filled with your details

**Subject** – you can add a topic here if you like, such as 'Homework'

**Send** – as soon as you press this the email you have been writing will be sent once the computer has linked to the ISP

**Reply** – if you highlight an email that you would like to reply to, you just click this button. The To box will automatically be filled, as well as the From box.

# Test your email: Send one!

To make sure that your email is working, send a test message. Double click on the email software icon and a window should appear. Click on the icon saying New Mail or New to open an email message window. Type in your own email address and press Send. If it is working properly you should be able to pick up this message in a few minutes by clicking on your Receive button.

## A group email

You can send a message to more than one person by entering as many names as you like into the To box. The same email will then go at the same time to all the e-pals entered.

## Address book

Some email packages have address books or contact details. You can enter all the email addresses of your friends. When you have filled in their details, all you'll need to do when you send an email is type in the name of your friend and their email address will automatically be entered into the box.

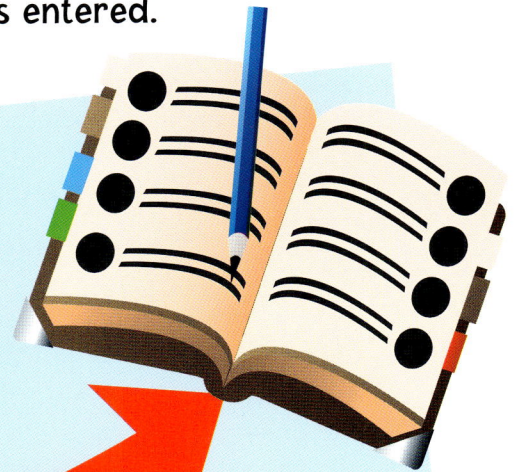

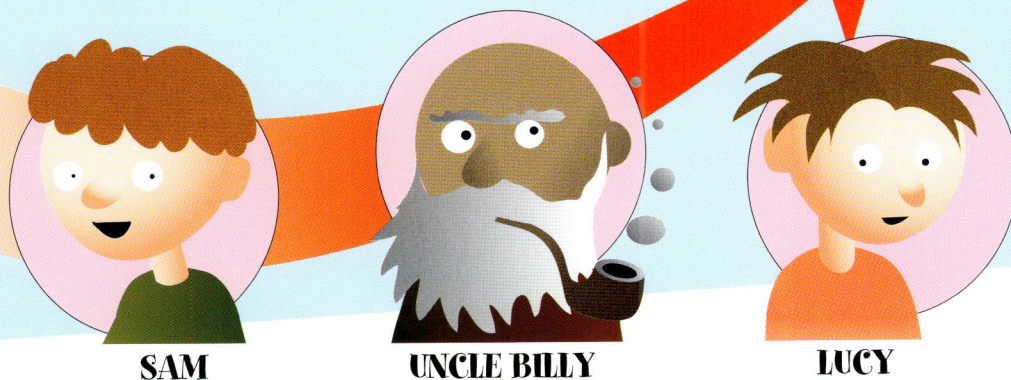

SAM          UNCLE BILLY          LUCY

# GETTING EMAIL

How you receive and organise your messages depends on your email package, but again there are some general hints and tips that you might find useful. To find out if you have mail, you must launch your email account which should automatically dial into your ISP. If there are any messages for you they will be downloaded and appear in your Inbox. Your Inbox will show who sent the message, what it is about (if they have put in a subject) and the time it was sent.

## Answering

If you want to reply to a mail, you just need to click on the Reply button either when the mail you are replying to is open or by highlighting the email in your Inbox and pressing Reply. There are some other option as well, if the email has been sent to lots of people, you can reply to all of them by clicking on a Reply All button. You can also send a message on to another person or group of people by forwarding it. Find the Forward button for this.

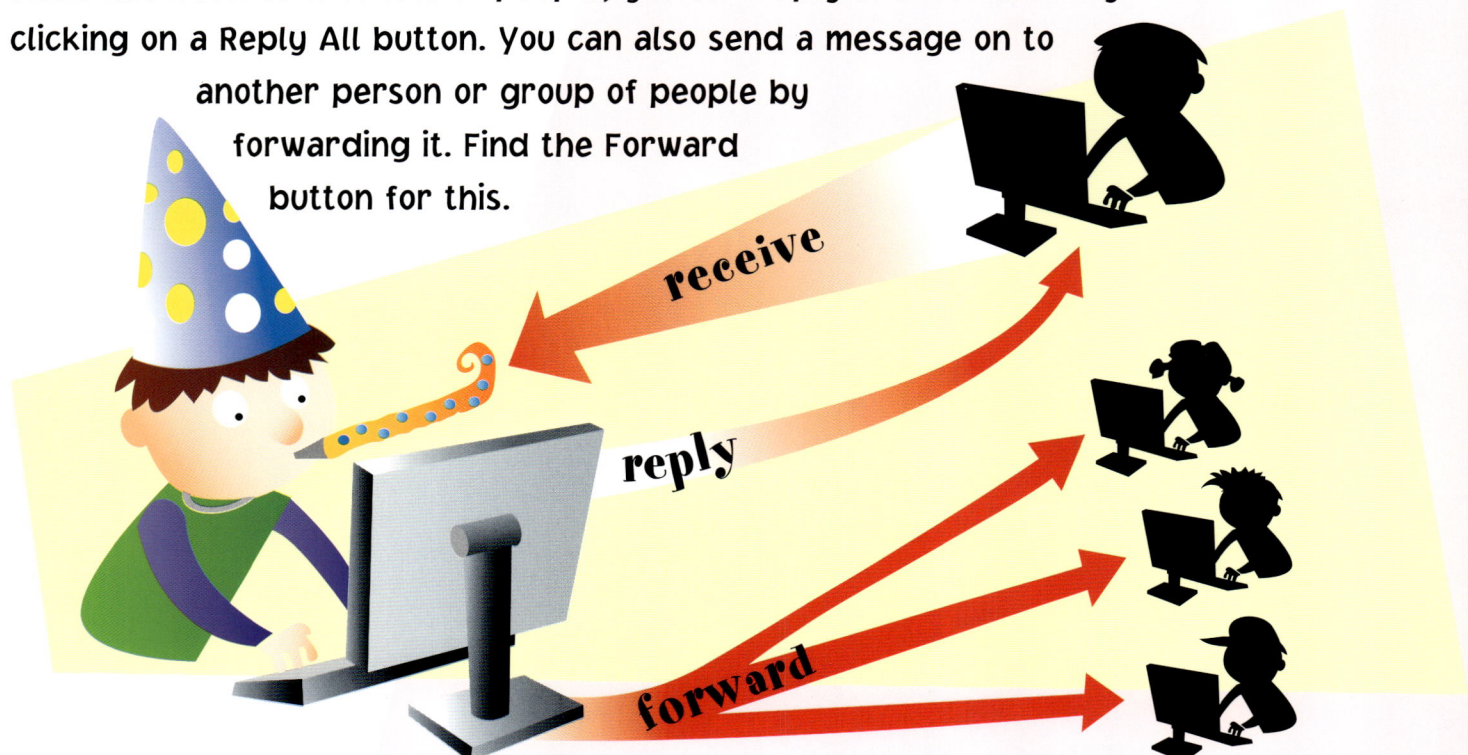

receive

reply

forward

# Organising Your messages

Every email package will have an Inbox. This is a folder which contains all your incoming emails. There is also an Outbox, which is where the emails you are sending sit until you have dialled up your email account. All the emails that you have ever sent can also stay on your computer in the Sent box.

## Your Inbox

The Inbox can get very crowded after a while and you might want to sort out emails. You can delete those you don't want to keep, but you might want to keep some. For these you can add folders to your email program which appear under your Inbox folder. You can name the folders by whatever you like – such as names of friends or subject matter.

INBOX

SAM

UNCLE BILLY

LUCY

## Working offline

Remember it is always better to write your mails offline, then dial up your account to send finished mails. This means that you are not 'on the phone' for a long time.

# ATTACHMENTS

If you were to send a letter to a friend and you wanted to add a little something to the letter, you could quite easily. Well, it's the same with email. You can add anything to your mail that can be stored on your computer as a file. And this added file is called an attachment.

## What can I attach?

You can add text files if you wanted, however, much more exciting would be pictures, sounds and movies. If you have these on your computer then they can be attached to your email.

There is one BIG warning though – the file that you send should not be very large. If you were to send a huge file, say about 1Mb, it could take ages to send from your computer and then take your friend ages to download.

## Sending an attachment

All email packages will differ slightly when it comes to attaching a file. If you are lucky you just drag a file onto the new email. Otherwise you have to find Insert File or Add Attachment in the drop down menus. This will open a dialog box asking you what file you would like to attach. Select the file and it will automatically be attached.

## It takes all kinds...

Files come in all kinds of formats – text, image, sound and so on. You can tell what kind of file they are by their file extension or by the icon.

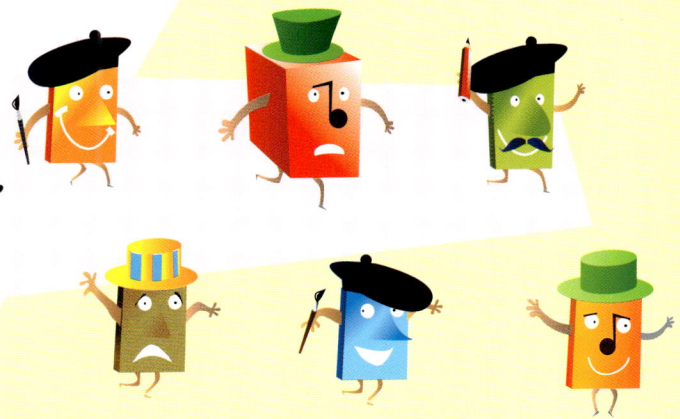

## Top tips

• remember that people have different computers, some have PCs with Windows, others have Macs. The file that you send as an attachment may not work, or be compatible, with all of them.

• try to make sure that the person you are sending an attachment to will be able to read it.

• make sure the attachment that you send is not too large, because it can take a long time to download a large file which is boring and expensive.

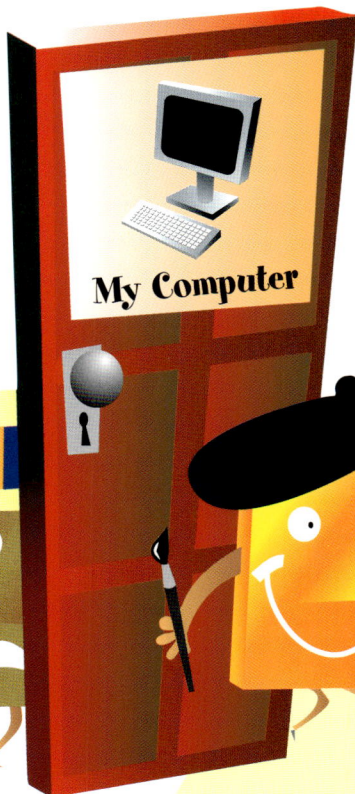

**My Computer**

## And the good news is...

The Great Ideas for Email CD is programmed to create attachments that most computers will read. The files are also small enough to be sent easily. The only software your e-pals will need are Quicktime™ and Shockwave™ – both of these are on the disc or free over the internet.

www.greatideasfor.co.uk

# BEWARE!

There are some things that every emailer should know when they send and receive emails. Firstly the practical side of sending mails, such as only going online when your emails are written and how big your attachment should be. Secondly, how to avoid being sent unwanted emails and viruses.

## Saving your phone bill

Some email packages will dial up your email account as soon as you open them. This means that from the moment you open them you are also on the telephone. You should be able to change this so that you only dial up when you have messages to send. Check either Options or Preferences for this. Only dialling when you have messages to send will mean that you are on the telephone line for seconds rather than minutes.

## Download time

If your file is large and your modem is not very fast you could be waiting for an hour before a file is downloaded. The more powerful your computer, modem and line, the faster the download time. But there is another alternative...

## ...Compression

You can get software that will squash file sizes and make them much much smaller. You just need to make sure that the person you are emailing can decompress, or expand, the squashed file. We have links on our website to the places where you can download compression software.

## Viruses

A virus is a tiny piece of computer programming that is designed to wreck your computer. The only scary thing about sending and receiving attachments is that this is how viruses can travel. Most viruses will appear as an attachment with a mail. The virus will not attack your computer unless you have opened the attachment. SO, never open any attachment that is on an email from someone you don't know, and only open attachments from friends if they have said that they are sending it. So BE WARNED!

## Virus protection

The best thing you could do to protect your computer would be to install virus detection software. We have links to the relevant sites on our website.

# E-PICTURES

Now instead of technical talk, here's the fun part. It's great to send a picture with your email so that your e-pal can see what you are talking about - your pet, your school, your family. There are lots of ways you can either make or find pictures too, so here goes...

## Photographs

There are a couple of ways that you can get photos onto your computer. If you are really hi-tech, you might have a digital camera. These just plug into the computer and will download the pictures you have taken. Easy. Secondly, you could scan photographs into the computer using a scanner. Make sure that you save your pictures as jpegs, this way they can be viewed by most computers.

## Clip art

You can buy CDs which have loads of pictures on them for you to use. Alternatively, you can find clip art on the internet. Try our Great Ideas for Email website – www.greatideasfor.co.uk – for places to find clip art. The pictures you'll find can be in various formats, from jpegs, bitmaps to picts and tifs. Jpegs are the most useful as they can be viewed by almost all computers.

## Drawing software

Some computers come with a Paint package which allows you to create your own pictures. You can also import pictures you have found and adapt them within the software. Then there are some very sophisticated drawing and design packages which are used by professionals, such as Photoshop®, Freehand® or Illustrator®.

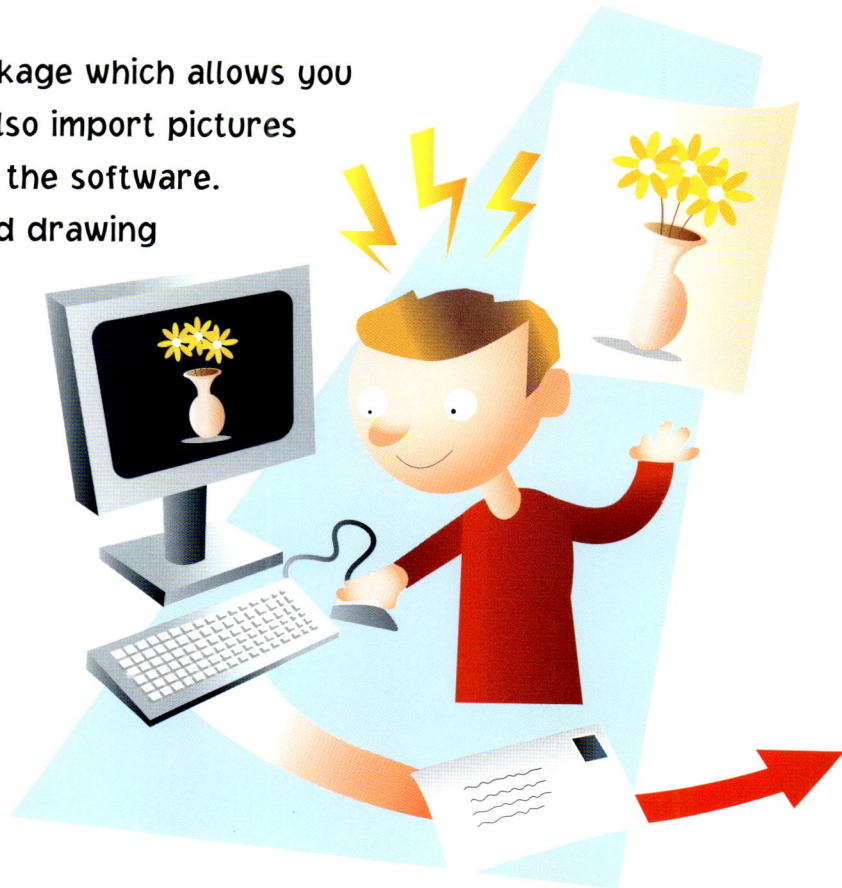

## E-pictures on the CD

If you don't have a drawing package on your computer or you are not sure how to use it, then try e-pictures on the CD. You can use the different-sized drawing tools to shape outlines and colour in. When you save the picture, it goes on to your hard disk and from there you can attach it to your email.

## Great Idea

Make a flip book with art created using the CD. By slightly adapting the artwork you have drawn, you could make a ball bounce or an eye wink, just by putting the printed art in sequence and flicking through it quickly.

# E-CARDS

Think of all the times you'll buy a card to send to a friend. You may be on holiday and want to send a postcard, or it may be a special occasion, such as a festival or birthday. It's great to receive cards through the post, but now you can make one that is much more personal, by designing it yourself and sending it by email.

## Speedy

Sending a card by post is now called SNAIL MAIL by techie people! The speed of sending an email cannot be matched by post – and it can save a few red faces if you have forgotten a birthday or celebration.

## Go surfing

If you go onto the website – www.greatideasfor.co.uk – you'll find links to sites that allow you to use their pictures to send as postcards over the internet.

## Stuff about e-cards

On the CD-ROM, you'll find an activity called e-cards. Here by dragging images onto a background you can design your own e-card. There is an area at the bottom of the screen which allows you to type in your special message.

## Saving your e-card

Once you are happy with your design and message, you can save the e-card onto your desktop by clicking the save button. The file is saved as a jpeg, which can easily be sent as an attachment to your email (see page 13).

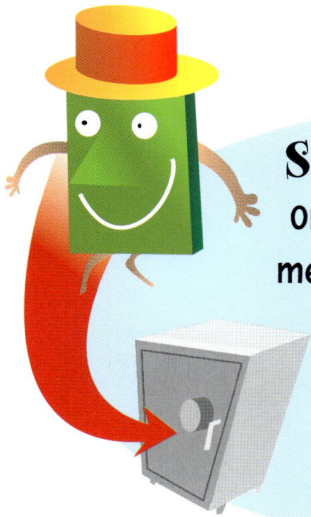

## Great Idea

Why not use the old system as well, and send a note through the post. Print out any pictures that you would like to use, colour them in and send in a decorated envelope. You could do chunky cards through the post by adding collage to your picture...

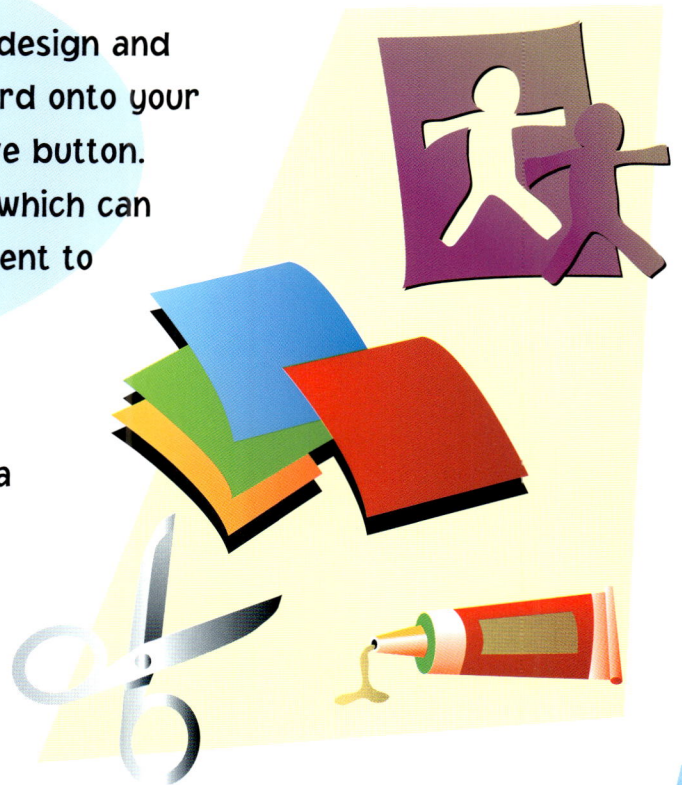

# E-CARTOONS

When you look at magazines and newspapers there are often black and white cartoon strips that make you laugh. Can you think of some of your favourites, perhaps Charlie Brown and Snoopy or Garfield? And then there are the longer comics such as Beano and X-men. How about creating your own and sending it to friends as an email?

## A one off

The cartoon strip has a complete story or joke in the series of pictures. To create one of these you need to think about the beginning, middle and end of the event, and the end needs to have some kind of punch line.

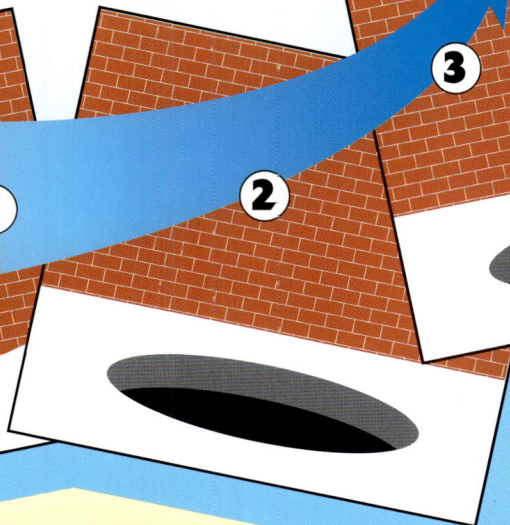

# What you can do

With our cartoon strip builder you can either use the images we have supplied in any order you like and just write into the speech bubbles, or you can draw your own. Try experimenting with different ideas, such as using the pencil to write into the window rather than using a speech bubble.

# A series

If you want to tell a longer story you could produce a story line that can be split into seven or more installments, like chapters. Each installment has four frames. So you can keep your e-pals entertained by giving them a new part of the story each day. All you need to remember is that you should leave each installment on a cliff-hanger, so that your e-pals will want to read the next installment!

# Surfing

Go to www.greatideasfor.co.uk to find links to comic sites which can give you loads of story line ideas and art styles.

So far we have described creative activities to do with words and pictures. Now imagine being able to play with music and sound. With our CD-ROM, you can compose your own tunes and send them to all your friends by email.

## Music from a computer?

If your computer has a CD-ROM drive, then it can definitely play music. If it has a microphone you could record music. But unless you have some special software, it won't let you write music.

## Composing

With our e-music activity, you can choose different instruments to play your composition. You can even have different instruments in the same tune. Experiment with the notes and instruments until you get something you like.

## Saving your tune

Once you have something you like, click on the Save button. The tune is saved as a midi file and can be played on all computers with a midi sound card. This should work on most computers, both Mac and PC. Other sound file formats include .wav and .aif, which are played by special multimedia software.

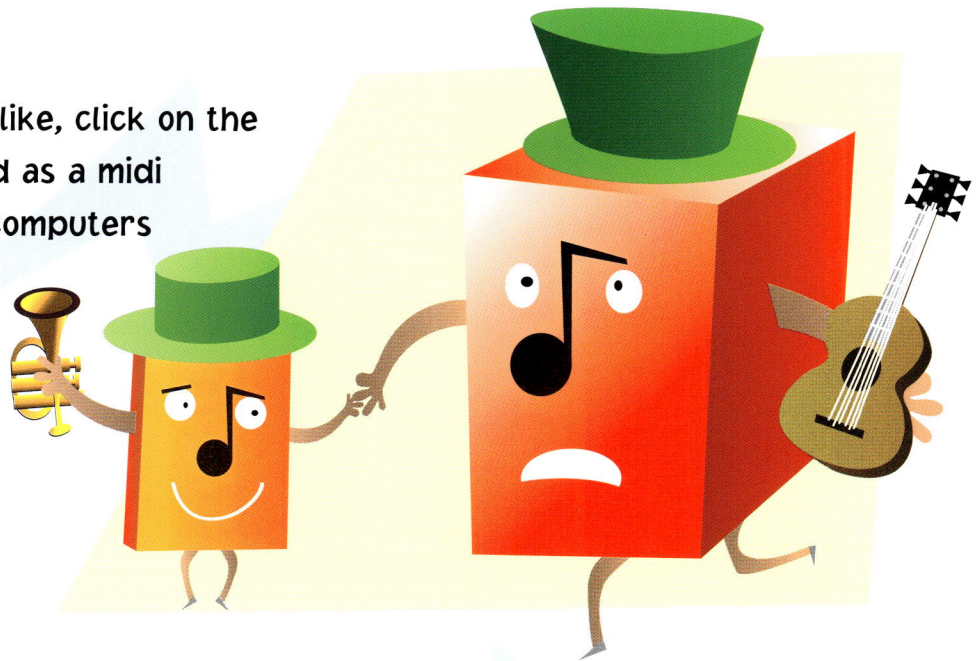

## Other sounds

If you have a microphone, you can record yourself talking or singing, or you could try and catch the dog barking, or the cat meowing...what else can you think of? You will need special sound editing software if you want to adapt the sound however, such as SoundEdit® or CoolEdit 2000.

## Go surfing

Head off to www.greatideasfor.co.uk to find links to sites that have lots of sounds you can download. You can even download songs to play...

Sending pictures and cards with your emails is great, but how about sending a challenge to a friend? Give them something to do and see if you can outwit them!

## Word puzzles

Click on e-puzzles on the CD. You'll find a grid for you to build up your own challenge. All you need to do is type words in to the column list. Once you have entered as many words as you want, press the fill button and all the squares in the grid will automatically fill. The words you have entered will be hidden in the grid, running forwards, backwards, diagonally, up or down.

## Saving your puzzle

Click on the save button to save your puzzle on to your desk top. The puzzle is saved as a jpeg which your e-pal can print out and complete.

## Quiz

Challenge your e-pal to a quiz. Write a series of questions on your email and see how many your e-pal gets right. If you want, you could give them multiple choice answers. Write your quiz directly into your email and send it off, they can answer in the email using capital letters which will make it easy to see their answers.

## Scavenger hunt

Why not set lots of your e-pals a scavenger hunt. This involves creating a list of digital objects you want your e-pals to collect from the internet. For example, you could ask for a picture of the planet Mars, the sound of a dog barking or the answer to a difficult question. Send the scavenger hunt off to your friends at exactly the same time and see who finds all these things first. They have to prove they have got them by emailing the objects to you!

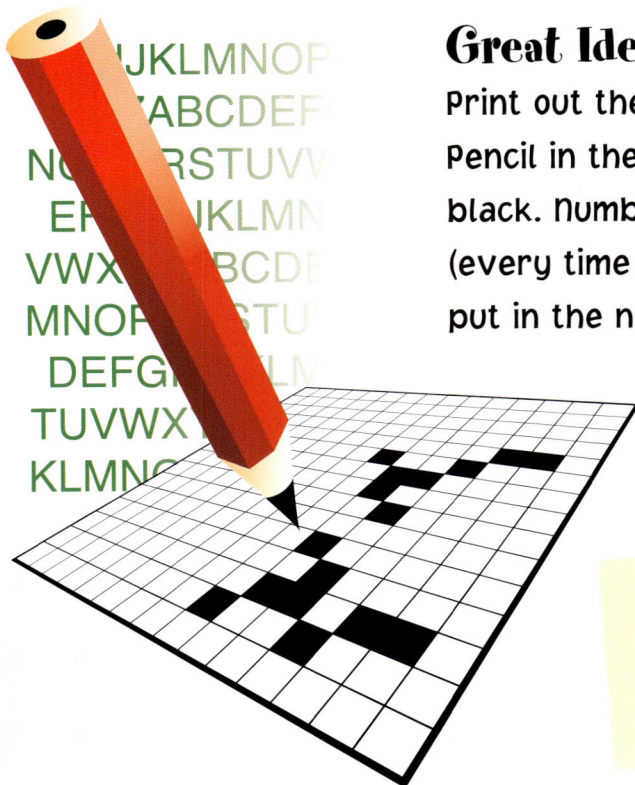

$X+2y(54b)=?$

## Great Idea

Print out the grid and use it to build a crossword. Pencil in the words, then colour all the blank squares black. Number the words from the top left along (every time you hit a new word either along or down put in the next number). Write a list of clues and try it out on an unsuspecting classmate.

## Surfing

Go to the website to find links to all kinds of puzzles on the internet.

www.greatideasfor.co.uk

# E-CODES

If you ever want to send a secret message then you need to work out some kind of code. Emails are great because you can put a password onto your email system so that no one else can read your messages...but you never know. So make doubly sure no one can pry by using a secret code.

## Make a coded message

Click on the e-code icon on the CD. You'll find a code wheel which will set messages for you in code automatically. All you have to do is set the wheel, so that the A you type will be represented by another letter. Remember that you'll have to let your e-pal know what A equals so that they can work out your message for themselves. This is the key for the code. You should try and send the key to the code secretly, for example, agreeing that the key letter will be the first letter of the email subject.

**A=E**

## Saving your e-code

When you click on save in e-codes the CD will automatically launch your default email program and your codec message will be in the message box. All you need to do is type in your e-pal's address - and remember to put the code key in as well.

## How about...

drawing a code system in e-pictures? All you need to do is draw pictures to match each letter of the alphabet. Send this as an attachment to your e-pal and print a copy for yourself. Then when you want to send a coded message, do it using e-pictures, drawing just the right images for each letter.

## Different codes

There's a great code called Railfence code which looks impossible to crack but is in fact very easy to create. Just write out your message, say: Meet at the park gates at eight. Write every other letter out on separate lines:

**MEATEAKAEAEGT**
**ETTHPRGTSTIH**

Now take the letters and put them on one line:

**MEATEAKAEAEGTETTHPRGTSTIH.** To make it even more difficult then write them out in groups of 4 letters like this:

**MEAT EAKA EAEG TETT HPRG TSTI H**.

To decipher this code you just need to split the letters in two and place one set under the other. If it doesn't come out right first time split the group again by one letter either way and see if it makes sense then.

## Surfing

On www.greatideasfor.co.uk there are links to sites which have coded messages for you to decipher, as well as information sites about the history of spies and their techniques.

A B C D E F G H I J K L M N O P Q R S T U V W X Y Z

There are games that you can play on the internet either by yourself or with a group of players, but you may not want to stay on-line for a long time. So here is a game that you can play with your e-pals that just requires email, all you will need is Shockwave®.

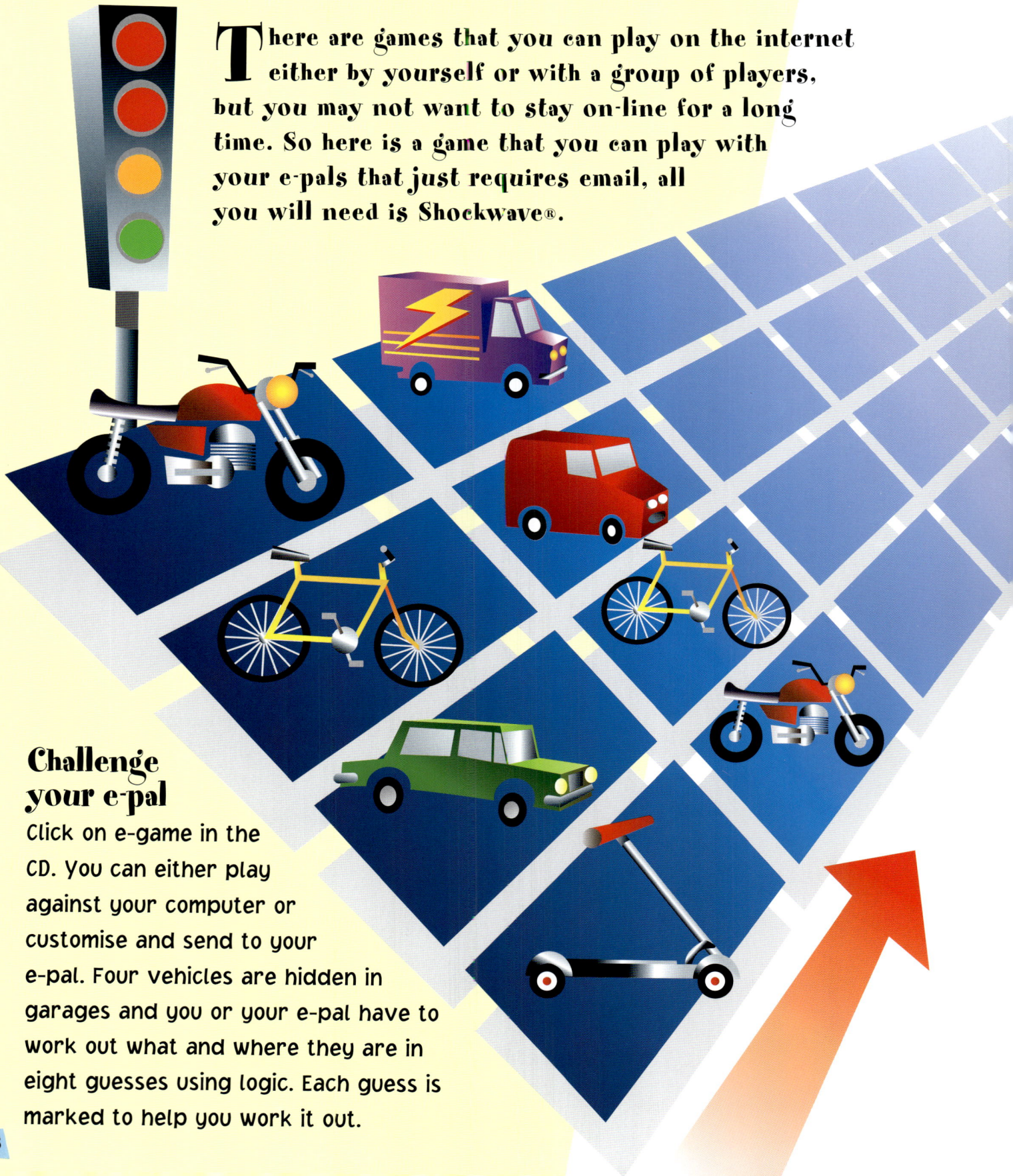

## Challenge your e-pal

Click on e-game in the CD. You can either play against your computer or customise and send to your e-pal. Four vehicles are hidden in garages and you or your e-pal have to work out what and where they are in eight guesses using logic. Each guess is marked to help you work it out.

## Saving your e-game

So that your e-pal can play the game, it is saved as a Shockwave file. This makes it interactive for both of you. You will need to have Shockwave on your machine and so will your e-pal, however, the good news is that it is on this disc for you to download if you don't have it, and on our website we have a link to the Shockwave site for you or your e-pal to download from there if preferred.

## Great Idea

Turn off the computer and play a card game instead. How about the memory game? Take a pack of cards and spread them on the floor face down. Then lift any two to see if they are the same number. If they are you have a pair, if not, keep lifting the cards in twos until all the pairs have been found.

## Surfing

We've found a whole heap of games for you to try over the internet, some that you can play by yourself and others that you play with other people on the internet. Go to www.greatideasfor.co.uk to find them.

# PROBLEMS

There are always things that can go wrong with your email system and with any piece of software. The best tip we can give is to keep a note of the telephone Helpline for all the software you have loaded onto your machine. So if you have trouble sorting out the problem yourself, you always have someone to call.

## However, before you resort to the telephone there are some things you could do first:

**1.** Check that all the cables going from your computer to the modem and from the modem to the telephone socket are secure and that the modem is switched on.

**2.** Make sure the user name and password that you are using are correct. Passwords must be exactly as they were keyed in, so you don't just check the spelling, you also need to check whether it was typed in with capital letters or not.

**3.** If emails are sent back to you without having reached their destination, it could be that you typed in the wrong email address. Sometimes, however, messages come back because the ISP you are using is having problems – be patient and try again in an hour or so.

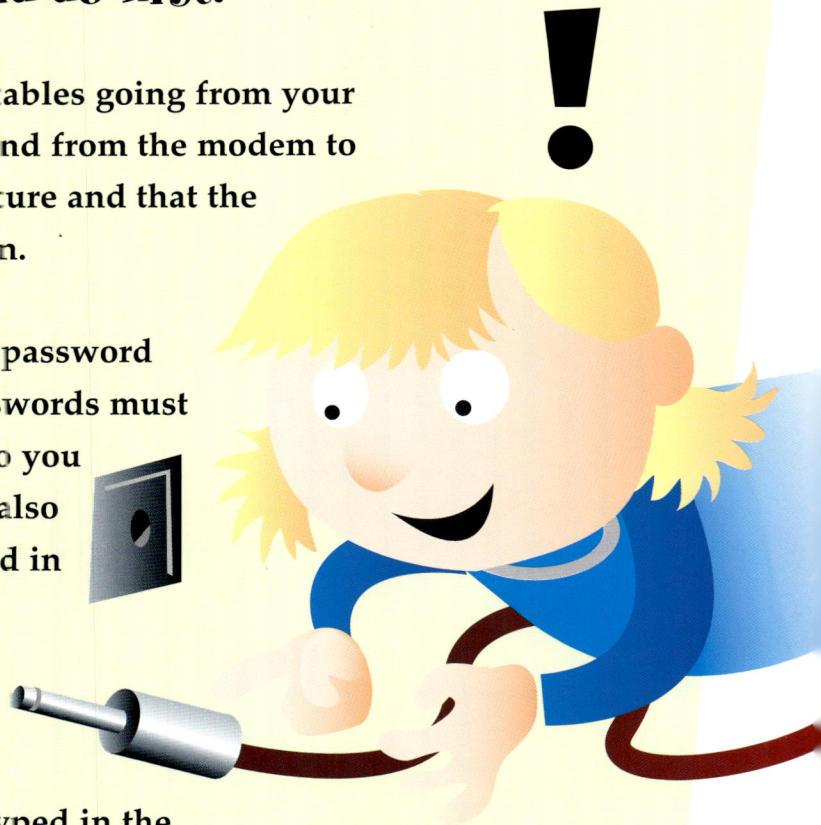

## Spam

If you have surfed the internet and entered your email address anywhere, you may receive what is called spam – this is like the junk mail that gets put through your mailbox at home. Sometimes you might be interested to read what it is about, but other times it is just annoying.

Check when you enter your email address that there is not a small box you can click on to make sure that you don't get spam. If it keeps coming, send an email back asking the sender to take you off their email address list.

## REMEMBER

If you meet someone for the first time via email, most of the time that is great. However, never give out your home address or telephone number to people you have only met online. You could find yourself emailing someone who may turn out to be a bit weird.

## Weird

If you do get an email that sounds a bit weird just delete it and never open anything from that person again. They'll soon get the message and leave you alone.

www.greatideasfor.co.uk

# GLOSSARY

**attachment**: any file that is sent with an email message. The file could be picture, sound or movie.

**browser**: software you need to explore the internet. Make sure you have the most up-to-date version.

**compatible**: there are hundreds of different software packages to use on Windows PCs and Macintoshs. If you have created a file in one piece of software, another computer may not be able to open it, because it does not have that software. This means the file is not compatible with the other computer. Some files can be read by lots of different software packages, these files are generally compatible with most machines.

**download**: when you copy emails or files onto your computer using your modem, you are downloading.

**file format**: every file created on any computer has a format that is made by the software you have used to create the file. When you save a document you are usually given choices for the kind of format you want to save your file as - make sure that it can be read by someone else's computer if you want it to send it.

**import**: when you are talking about technology, import means putting one file inside another. For example, if you want to put a picture into a text file, you import it. In the file menus of different software you will find the word Import or Insert, and this command will allow you to bring in another file.

**internet**: a worldwide network of computers connected together by telephone. You need a modem and special software to connect it up.

**Internet Service Provider (ISP)**: the software you need to get you onto the internet. The ISP holds the phone number you dial to get access to all the computers linked to the internet - their powerful computers connect you to computers in the network.

**jpeg**: a file format for a picture. This format can be used within most software packages, and can be viewed using your internet browser.

**midi**: a file format for sound. This format can be heard by opening it using Quicktime™ or your browser.

**modem**: a piece of hardware that connects your computer to the telephone line. Computers today often have internal modems, so you don't need to buy it as an extra.

**offline**: if you are not connected to the internet you are offline.

**online**: if you are connected through your phone line to the internet you are online.

**scanner**: a piece of hardware that turns a picture or photograph into a digital image. It works a bit like a photocopier, but instead of the copy being on paper it goes on to the computer.

**software**: a set of instructions that tell a computer what to do.

**virus**: a nasty program that gets into your computer without you knowing and can destroy your files.

## Secret Extras on the CD

Go to E-music - we have put in some hidden extras just to give you more fun:-

1. If you wanted another instrument sound, press down your Alt button and click onto an instrument button, you will get a drop down menu from which you can choose over 100 different instrument sounds. The instrument sound will always go back to our choice when you leave the activity.

2. If you wanted to hear your tune without one particular instrument playing, press down the Shift button and click the instrument you want to silence. To hear that instrument again, press Shift and click again. The cross should disappear and the instrument play again.

3. Finally if you want your tune to play faster or slower, hold down the shift button and use your up and down arrows to make it faster or slower. The tune you save will play with the speed you have set using these buttons.